Sunny and Sassy
~Come Out of the Wild~

"The Story of Two Real-life Chincoteague Ponies"

Written by Suzanne T. Immen

~

Illustrated by Nikita Garets

Copyright © 2016 by Suzanne T. Immen

All right reserved.
This book or any portion
thereof may not be reproduced or used in
any manner whatsoever without the express
written permission of the publisher except
for the use of brief quotations in a book
review.

Printed in the United States of America

First Printing, 2016.

Grayce Wynds Farm Publishing
2450 Grayce Wynds Drive
Supply, NC   28462
www.graycewyndsfarm.com

Dedication

This book is dedicated to my husband Bill and granddaughter Alice Paige Leland. Together, we all three shared the adventure!!

Acknowledgments

The author wishes to thank the following people:

~Husband Bill for always being ready for a wild horse adventure

~Toya Wilson-Smith for being a wonderful teacher, adviser, mentor, and friend

~Debbie Ober, Chincoteague Pony Rescue, for all of her help with Sunny and Jess and for all of her insights she shared about the Chincoteague pony penning "experience"

~Kelly Lidard, professional photographer, writer, and Chincoteague pony enthusiast for sharing her one-of-a-kind photographs

~Max Kuchin for his invaluable help in formatting the manuscript for final printing

~Angie Alaya, graphic artist, for her collaboration in designing the book cover

It was a lovely day in May when Shashay Lady gave birth to Jess. They were off to themselves and all alone. Like most new foals, Jess wobbled, stood up, looked around, and started running. Whee!!

It was a hot day in July when Dove gave birth to Sunny. They, too, were off by themselves. Sunny wobbled and knew right where to find his mother's milk to drink. In no time, he raced away from his mom to run right up to Surfer Dude, his dad.

"They look so much alike," she thought with love.

Both boys stayed close to their mothers but started playing with other foals, too. They drank milk, ate grasses, and drank water when their dads herded them to the water holes. Dads were the bosses! Jess liked to run around and bite everyone. He thought it was fun, but his mom finally bit him back. "Ouch!"

Both boys lived on Assateague Island where they roamed around wherever they wanted to go. They were wild but didn't know it. Sometimes, they noticed odd two-legged horses watching them. Some of them floated in the water in strange-looking things called boats. Their moms told them to stay away from them because they weren't horses at all. They were people! The boys were careful, but Jess was still curious. He wasn't afraid!

One day, things got really weird. People were sitting on the backs of horses and riding around, waving their arms and making all kinds of noises. All of the wild horses moved away from them.

"Stay close!" said Dove.

"Stay close!" said Shashay Lady.

Sunny and his mother were members of the southern herd while Jess and his mother lived in the northern herd. To stay away from the loud people, the northern herd moved down the beach. The people on horses stayed all around them and guided them as they moved along. As they moved down the beach, Jess danced in the ocean waves. He loved this adventure. There were people everywhere watching him.

Both mothers knew what was going to happen. "We are going inside fences with the other horses. Don't be scared, the people will feed us. Then, tomorrow, you are going swimming. It is a long swim so get your rest when we get inside."

Once inside, Jess looked through the fence and looked straight into the eyes of Sunny. Both boys came close and breathed into each others' nostrils. However, it didn't seem like a time to play.

"Yikes!" said Sunny. "This is scary, don't you think? I was told to stay away from the two-legged horses, but they are everywhere. And there is no more room to run."

"Scary?" said Jess. "I think this is an awesome adventure. My mom says we are going swimming tomorrow. I will race you!" Sunny shook his head and walked away. He didn't know about that crazy boy!

A little later, the boys were indeed tired. Sunny closed his eyes and dozed. When he woke up, his mother had moved. He walked around with nervous eyes, looking everywhere, when he spotted his dad. Surfer Dude was majestic, and all his mares, including his mother, huddled close to him.

Jess got one of those deep sleeps. When he awoke, for once, he was quiet. He stayed close to his mother who stayed close to his dad, Tornado's Prince of Tides. He wasn't quite so bold now. That kid on the other side of the fence seemed so weak. What if he didn't make it?

The mothers nursed their boys and tried to prepare them for what they knew was coming. They told the boys that in the morning the large combined herd would start moving towards the water, and then they would be herded into the channel to swim to the other side. Sunny was quiet, listening to his mother and trying to understand. Jess simply said, "I am a good swimmer, Mom. It will be fun, right?" Shashay smiled tenderly at her energetic son. She told herself that he, of all the foals, would be fine. He was fearless!

Later that night, Sunny leaned against his mother. "Why do we have to do this, Mama? I don't know how to swim."

"I know, Honey. You are only a few weeks old. So little and so sweet! When you are in the water, though, pretend you are running. You will start running in the water. I am not worried about it. Trust me!" She pressed her head against his side, and a tear trickled down her face. She had done this before.

Sure enough! The next morning, the people called "saltwater cowboys" started riding around, hollering, and making loud snapping noises. Sunny and Jess, along with all the horses, wanted to get away from them. They came to the channel and plunged into the water. Jess yelled "whee!!" while Sunny just ran with all his might. What an experience!

Sunny and Jess were swimming. They were surrounded by all the other horses who were swimming, too. People were everywhere in boats and on the shore.

"Here they come! The horses are coming! Look at them! Wow! That is amazing!" The people cheered with excitement.

The horses looked straight ahead, going as fast as they could to get to the other shore. Sunny and Jess and all the other foals just tried to keep their heads above water. They didn't know what was going on! Sunny remembered that his mother told him to run in the water just like he did on land.

When they climbed out on the other shore, all the foals were exhausted and dripping wet, but they had made it. Nothing seemed right any more...until they found their mothers.

"What happens now, Mom?" asked Jess.

"Son, hold your head high because we are going to parade down Main Street. We will be surrounded by people, and they will cheer for us."

"Cheer for us? What does that mean?"

Shashay Lady laughed. "They are telling us that we are beautiful, and they love us. They think we are amazing and special."

Jess said, "Well, then, I shall trot with my tail up—just to show them."

"You mean, to show off, huh?"

Jess smiled and bumped his mother with his nose. As always, he bumped her hard. That boy!!

Little Sunny felt foggy in the head. Things were happening so fast, he didn't know what to think. He felt his mother's breath as she found him.

"See? I told you that you would have no trouble swimming. You kept up with all of us. You are small but mighty. Just like your father."

Sunny leaned on his mother. He was tired. He knew he was the smallest one in the whole herd. He just wanted to lie down and rest..... which is just what he did. This time, Dove stood over him to protect him. She wouldn't let any other horse step on her sweet baby.

"Haw!! Git up!! Move on out!" The Saltwater Cowboys were at it again, herding the horses to make them trot down Main Street. The pavement was hard and hot as the band of horses moved swiftly at the commands. Crowds of people waved and shouted along the road. All the noise and crowds made the horses feel nervous—even Jess! He kept his eyes on the horses straight ahead of him. Go, go, go! Sunny was lost amongst the mass of moving horses. He was filled with fear, but he did his best to keep up with them.

Sunny knew he was lost. The parade was over, and somehow he found himself inside fences again with the large, sweaty herd. He just stood there, wondering how he was going to find his mother. He watched as other horses walked around him, looking for their families and food and water. He heard the fearful calls of other foals, looking for their mothers. He just froze, hoping his mother would find him. As he looked around, waiting, he saw his dad. Without taking his eyes off of him, he started moving quickly. He was little, but he was determined. His small size made it possible for him to dodge in and out of the other horses. When Surfer Dude and Dove saw him coming, they neighed so loudly that everyone knew....Sunny had been found.

Jess heard the neighing over on the other side of the pen. He was chomping hay and enjoying himself. He didn't exactly know what was going on, but he liked it. He started to go find Sunny, but he heard his mother tell him to stay close.

"But, Mom," he wailed, "I want to go play." He danced around a bit, but she didn't smile.

"Jess, do you see that little feller walking around, crying? It is easy to get lost in here. Stay close!"

Evening finally settled on the big corral with the big herd inside. The horses were being held in the fairgrounds of the town called Chincoteague. There was plenty of food to eat, carnival rides, and a band playing dance music, but the herd got quiet as many dozed or even laid down. Jess wondered where Sunny was. He couldn't see him, but he missed him. Sunny leaned against his mother. What a day! He wanted to go back to Assateague Island. Both mothers closed their eyes as they began to say goodbye to their little boys.

Later that night, the Saltwater Cowboys were everywhere. Slapping numbers on the rear ends of the foals and writing down the names of their parents. Some of the foals were kickers, but the cowboy who numbered Sunny thought he was so cute, he gave him his first scratch. Nice! Dove watched carefully. Jess saw what was happening and shoved his behind right up to a cowboy who pushed him away. "You aren't going to kick me, Big Guy."

Jess thought to himself, "No, I wasn't going to kick you. I was trying to help you. I was hoping for a good scratch, too!"

The next morning, it started all over again. Cowboys were everywhere, rounding up mares and foals and herding them into an enclosure. Then they chased them around a chute. The mothers raced ahead of their babies while the babies were trapped in small holding pens. Before they knew what happened to them, the foals were all bunched up together, and their mothers were gone—separated from them. All of the foals began to holler. Sunny and Jess were just as loud and scared as all the others. From a distance, their mothers hollered back. They were saying goodbye.

Jess looked around at all the foals and saw Sunny, huddled in the corner — the smallest one of all. "Hey, kid, how ya doing?" Sunny looked around and saw the crazy boy.

"I want my mama," was all he said.

Jess felt sorry for him. "Aw, we have to grow up sometime. We'll be OK."

He didn't know that Sunny was going to be his brother. Sunny stood really still, looking off in the distance. His mother once told him that he had the "eye of the eagle." Sunny wondered what she meant by that, but he kinda liked it. Today, he could see her in his mind, standing in the wind on Assateague with her mane and tail blowing about her. She was beautiful.

"Where is Number Three?" a cowboy called out.

"In here," was the reply.

Before he knew it, Sunny was wrangled out of his little band of foals and guided into the sunlight. The noise of the loudspeaker and colors and smells terrified him. He raised up to bolt, but the big cowboys had him hemmed up. There was more hollering as they made him face this way and then that way. Then, all of sudden, they were taking him back to the pen. What in the world was that all about?

"Where is Number Twelve?" a cowboy called out. "Here he is—another colt."

Jess was caught and held just like Sunny. He was thinking to himself, "get your hands off of me! I am getting out of here. I am stronger than you." And sure enough, he bucked and reared, and then he bucked and reared some more. Another cowboy showed up to lend assistance. That Jess was a feisty one! However, in the end, he was paraded around just like little Sunny, and he, too, was soon delivered back to his pen. What in the world was that all about?

Mama Sue and her granddaughter Paige hugged each other with sheer happiness. They had just bought two Chincoteague ponies at the auction. Number Three and Number Twelve!!!! They had been to the payment booth twice where Mama Sue wrote checks to pay for her wild babies. All kinds of people said "congratulations, Ladies" which made Mama Sue and Paige hug each other again. Daddy Bill found them and joined in the hugging. "Let's go find those boys."

"I am going to tell them that I love them," said Paige. And she did.

Jess and Sunny and the other foals had calmed down a bit. They somehow knew that the two-legged horses were in charge of them. They didn't feel free any more. All of the foals seemed to know that their lives would never be the same, but hay and water helped them to feel better. Mama Sue, Daddy Bill, and Paige hung over the railings, trying to touch the babies. "We are proud parents of two beautiful boys," said Mama Sue with a smile. "Yep!" said Paige. "Yep!" said Daddy Bill.

"Number Three, look at us, Baby." Sunny heard his new family, calling to him. Was he Number Three? He looked at the people and kept on munching.

"Number Twelve, look at us, Baby." Jess heard his new family, calling to him. Was he Number Twelve? He looked at the people and took a drink of water.

Things continued to get stranger and stranger for the foals. One by one they were taken out of the pens and taken away. By 3:00 the next day, Sunny and Jess were alone in their pens. They stood by each other, looking at each other through the slats.

"Come on, you two!! Your new parents are here to take you to your new home. Your Assateague days are over, fellas!" the Saltwater Cowboy said.

Of course, Sunny and Jess could not imagine what he were talking about. Once outside, there were those same people. They put their arms around the boys and just stood there. That was weird! Sunny and Jess got their pictures taken and got their first kisses!!! What in the world? Then, they were put in a box with five other foals, and the door was slammed shut. At least there was hay and water inside. Sunny was little and crowded through the bigger kids to get his share. He was learning already! He had to take care of himself. His mother was nowhere to be seen—or his famous dad.

The big metal box and foals started swaying as the horse trailer pulled out onto the road, soon leaving behind the quaint little town of Chincoteague. The boys and other foals were being taken to a farm in Maryland where they would live for the next ten months, growing and learning how to live with people.

Mama Sue, Paige, and Daddy Bill promised Miss Debbie to come see their new babies before they returned home to North Carolina. Sunny and Jess heard Mama Sue talk about sending her babies to "boarding school." The next day, sure enough! There were those same people again. They tried to touch Sunny and Jess to rub them. The boys kinda liked it, but they were scared too. They remembered that their mothers had said to stay away from them.

Daddy Bill said, "Boys, Miss Debbie will take good care of you. We are building you a home far away from here in North Carolina. When we get finished, we will come back to get you....and we will always be your family. You boys are a gift from God!"

Later that night, when the barn got really quiet and dark, Sunny and Jess snuggled up close to each other. "We are going to be brothers," said Jess.

"What is a brother?" asked Sunny.

"Best friends," answered Jess. "And we will live together forever with our new mama and new daddy." Somehow....the boys weren't so scared anymore, and they knew they would be OK. They both were glad to be alive, and they smiled, thinking about their new life together. So far, so good!!!!

Photographs of Sunny and Jess Coming Out of the Wild

Baby Sunny with mother (Dove) and father (Surfer Dude)

Baby Sunny with mother

Baby Sunny on the island

Jess on the day he was born, May 27, 2014

Baby Jess in the wild

Baby Jess on the island

Baby Jess following mother (Shashay Lady)

Jess in the holding pen after first round up

Surfer Dude and his family in holding pen before the swim

Jess herded down to the water for the swim

The parade down Main Street

Sunny and mother (Dove) after the parade

Lost baby after the parade
(he finally found his mother)

Pens holding the foals for the auction

Sunny being sold at auction

Sunny being auctioned

Jess being sold at auction

Sunny, Mama Sue, and Paige
(with a Saltwater Cowboy)

Jess, Mama Sue, and Paige
(with a Saltwater Cowboy)

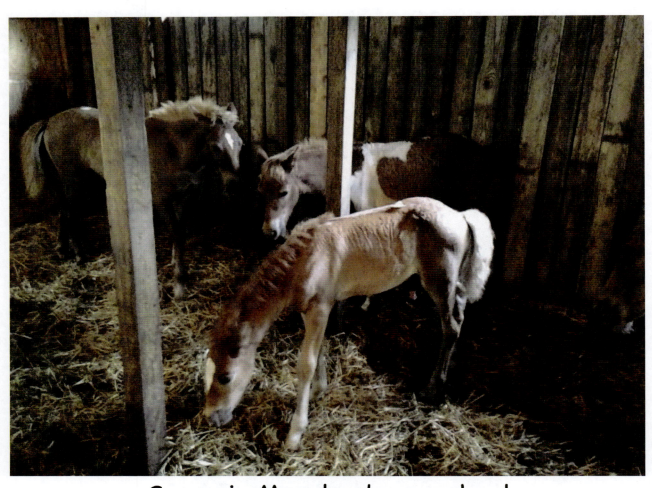
Sunny in Maryland pre-school

Jess in Maryland pre-school

Made in the USA
Charleston, SC
25 July 2016